Timba the
Tiger

by Jan Latta

Reading consultant: Susan Nations, M.Ed., author/literacy coach/consultant in literacy development

Science and curriculum consultant: Debra Voege, M.A., science and math curriculum resource teacher

GARETH**STEVENS**

GS

PUBLISHING

A Member of the WRC Media Family of Companies

Hello! My name is Timba, and I am a tiger. I live
in India with my mother and my baby sister. Our
mother goes to the forest to hunt food for us.

Meet Tara, my baby sister. When she was born, she weighed just 2 pounds (1 kilogram). Our mom will take care of us until we are about two years old. Then we will go off on our own to live and hunt.

Tigers have different ways of **communicating** with each other. When we smell another tiger, we make faces! We lift back our head, open our mouth, and wrinkle our nose.

We make lots of noises. We pant, growl, cry, hiss, scream, snarl, purr, and of course, roar.

We also communicate with odor. We leave our scent by spraying urine on trees. With just one sniff, tigers can tell who was in the area.

We also rub up against or hug trees to leave our scent.

We scratch tree trunks, too. Our claw marks let other tigers know this is our home **territory**.

We are very good swimmers, but we do not like to get our faces wet.

Just like house cats, tigers like to play with and **groom** each other.

We spend most of the day sleeping or resting. When the Sun begins to set, we get ready to hunt. We do most of our hunting at night.

Tigers walk on the soft pads of their toes. Walking softly helps us sneak up on our **prey**.

Our footprints are called **pug marks**. We have five toes on our front feet and four on our back feet. Can you see my pug mark?

Tigers are built to hunt. Sharp teeth line our powerful jaws. Our eyesight is good, and we have a strong sense of smell.

We have great hearing too! See the white spots behind my mom's ears? My sister and I can follow her through the tall grass by watching those spots.

To catch prey, our mom must sneak up on it. She crouches down on her belly and crawls very slowly. It can take her as long as thirty minutes to cover a short distance.

Then she **charges** on an animal and pounces! She cannot always catch her prey, however. She catches an animal one time in about twenty tries.

Tigers are **carnivores**, which means we eat meat. We can eat up to 77 pounds (35 kg) of meat at one time.

No wonder we are the biggest of the big cats! A full-grown male can weigh 660 pounds (300 kg). Females are about half as big as males.

We each have our home territory, which we use for hunting. Males cover an area of about 40 square miles (100 square kilometers). Females cover an area about half as big. Some males will share the territory of many females.

Every tiger has a different pattern of stripes than any other tiger. Look closely. Can you tell the difference between each tiger?

My **ancestors** have lived on Earth for about two million years. At one time, there were eight different kinds of tigers. Over the last fifty years, three of those kinds have died out. Every day, humans destroy our **habitat** by building towns, roads, and farms. Every day, more tigers die.

Today, there are only about five thousand tigers living in the wild. We need help to **survive** if the roar of the wild tiger is still to be heard.

Tiger Facts

Did You Know?

• Tigers can live in jungles or meadows. They can even live on snowy mountains, in swamps, or in river valleys.

• A tiger's fangs can be 3 inches (7.6 centimeters) long. Its claws can be as long as 4 inches (10 cm).

• In the dark, tigers can see six times better than humans.

• A tiger's stripes never change as it grows.

• People have put lions and tigers together in zoos. A tigon has a tiger for a dad and a lion for a mom. A liger has a lion for a dad and a tiger for a mom. Ligers are much bigger than tigons.

• Tigers can pull the same amount of weight that it would take thirty people to pull.

• Tigers will eat prey as small as grasshoppers and as big as elephants. They will even eat prey as dangerous as crocodiles!

• After eating part of its large prey, a tiger will bury what is left. It does not want other animals to eat it. The next day, the tiger digs up the leftovers to eat.

• Tigers must hunt at least once per week.

• Most adult tigers live and hunt alone.

• Humans hunt tigers. Wild dogs, elephants, and bears hunt tiger cubs.

• Tigers live up to twenty years in the wild. In zoos or protected areas, they can live as long as twenty-five years.

• Today, there are more tigers living in zoos than in the wild.

Map — Where Tigers Live

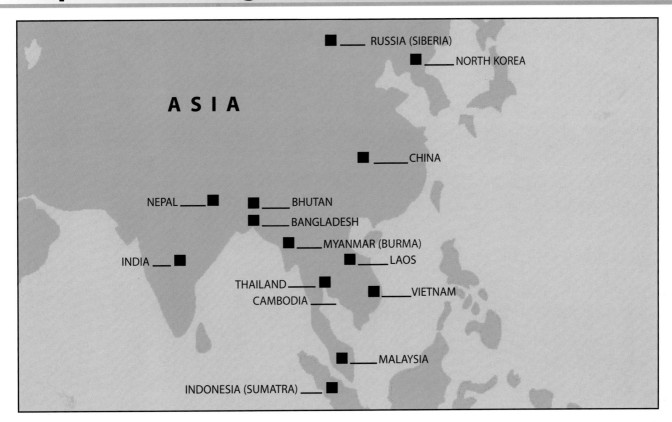

Glossary

ancestors — relatives that lived long before one's parents were born

carnivores — meat eaters

charges — runs toward something very fast to attack it

communicating — sending messages to others

groom — to lick, brush, and clean

habitat — the environment, or place, where an animal lives

prey — animals that are hunted

pug marks — the footprints of a large wild cat

survive — to live

territory — the area that an animal lives in and claims as its own

More Information

Books

Amazing Tigers! I Can Read Book 2 (series). Sarah L. Thomson (HarperTrophy)

A Tiger Grows Up. Wild Animals (series). Anastasia Suen (Picture Window Books)

Tigers. All About Wild Animals (series). Catherine Gardner, ed. (Gareth Stevens Publishing)

Web Sites

Kid's Planet: Tiger Fact Sheet
www.kidsplanet.org/factsheets/tiger.html
Get fun facts about tigers.

National Geographic Cyber Tiger
www.nationalgeographic.com/features/97/tigers/maina.html
On this site, you get to be the zookeeper and set up a tiger's habitat!

Publisher's note to educators and parents: Our editors have carefully reviewed these Web sites to ensure that they are suitable for children. Many Web sites change frequently, however, and we cannot guarantee that a site's future contents will continue to meet our high standards of quality and educational value. Be advised that children should be closely supervised whenever they access the Internet.

Please visit our Web site at: www.garethstevens.com
For a free color catalog describing Gareth Stevens Publishing's list of high-quality books and multimedia programs, call 1-800-542-2595 (USA) or 1-800-387-3178 (Canada). Gareth Stevens Publishing's fax: (414) 332-3567.

Library of Congress Cataloging-in-Publication Data

Latta, Jan.
   Timba the tiger / by Jan Latta. — North American ed.
      p. cm. — (Wild animal families)
   Includes bibliographical references.
   ISBN-13: 978-0-8368-7772-4 (lib. bdg.)
   ISBN-13: 978-0-8368-7779-3 (softcover)
   1. Tigers—Juvenile literature. I. Title.
   QL737.C23L366   2007
   599.756—dc22   2006032129

This North American edition first published in 2007 by
Gareth Stevens Publishing
A Member of the WRC Media Family of Companies
330 West Olive Street, Suite 100
Milwaukee, WI 53212 USA

This U.S. edition copyright © 2007 by Gareth Stevens, Inc.
Original edition and photographs copyright © 2005 by Jan Latta.
First produced as *Adventures with Timba the Tiger* by
TRUE TO LIFE BOOKS, 12b Gibson Street, Bronte, NSW 2024 Australia

Acknowledgements: The author thanks Jon Resnick who generously allowed reproduction of his photographs on pages 8, 9, and 17.

Project editor: Jan Latta
Design: Jan Latta

Gareth Stevens editorial direction: Valerie J. Weber
Gareth Stevens editor: Tea Benduhn
Gareth Stevens art direction: Tammy West
Gareth Stevens Graphic designer: Scott Krall
Gareth Stevens production: Jessica Yanke and Robert Kraus

Printed in Canada

1 2 3 4 5 6 7 8 9 10 10 09 08 07 06